HAPPINESS

for my children

HarperCollins*Publishers*
77–85 Fulham Palace Road,
Hammersmith, London W6 8JB

www.harpercollins.co.uk

Published by HarperCollins*Publishers* 2007
1

A catalogue record for this book
is available from the British Library

ISBN-10 0 00 725436 9
ISBN-13 978 0 00 725436 1

Printed in Italy by Lego SpA

HAPPINESS

Let us be lovely
And let us be kind
Let us be silly and free
It won't make us famous
It won't make us rich
But damnit how HAPPY we'll be!

LET US BE LOVELY

BEAUTIFUL THOUGHTS

The HOPPY HOPPY SPARROW plants beautiful thoughts that grow like FLOWERS in the BLACKNESS of SPACE

Note

Oh that the World were full of Hoppy Hoppy Sparrows

Let us remember that in this RICH and BEAUTIFUL world there are only 2 things worth living for —

LOVE and HAPPINESS*

*oh ok, and maybe CHOCOLATE ▦

LOVE and HAPPINESS

The SHEEP of DESTINY

He SMILES because he sees your future.

And Oh, how HAPPY shall that future be!

May its gentle RAIN of HAPPINESS fall soft upon your head

The CLOUD of JOY

HAPPINESS

At the centre of the BIG YELLOW CIRCLE is a TINY GOLDEN DISK. Sometimes we are VERY NEAR that CENTRE. Sometimes we are OH SO FAR AWAY.

He knows not where he's going
For the ocean will decide –
It's not the DESTINATION...

...It's the glory of THE RIDE

ZEN DOG

That STILL and SETTLED Place

In that STILL and SETTLED place
There's nobody but you
You're where I BREATHE my oxygen
You're where I SEE my view
And when the World feels full of noise
My HEART knows what to do
It finds that STILL and SETTLED place
And DANCES there with YOU

WARNING

v. powerful

Please use wisely

HAPPINESS VIBES

The BISCUIT TIN of LIFE

RICH TEA BISCUIT   LUXURY CHOCOLATE FINGER

Just as the RICH TEA BISCUIT lives in HARMONY with the LUXURY CHOCOLATE FINGER, so should we all live in HARMONY together in the great Assorted Biscuit Tin that we call LIFE

"Why do you fly outside the box?"

"I fly outside the box because I can."

"But we KNOW the box. We are SAFE inside the box."

"That, my friend, is why I leave it. For YOU may be SAFE...

...but I AM FREE!"

The BUTTERFLY of FREEDOM

The HAPPY POTATO

He LIVES his life like a slow
and joyful DANCE upon the SAND

Nobody knew what it WAS or where it had COME FROM but such was its POWER that it leaked and seeped from person to person until the WHOLE WORLD was infected by its BEAUTY

The LOVELINESS

THE PIG OF HAPPINESS

he is <u>so</u> happy

May his JOYFUL SMILE remind
us how much there is to be
HAPPY about

THE END